Classic Children's Literature

**Practice Handwriting
with Excerpts from the Great Books**

Classic Copywork: Print **Vol. 3**

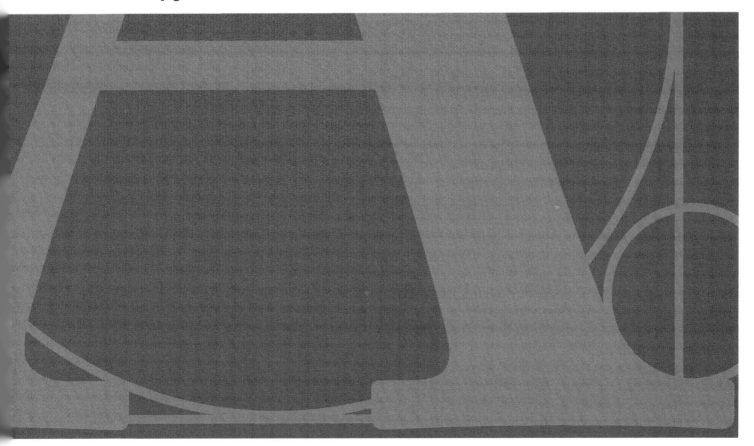

ISBN: 0692627863
ISBN-13: 978-0692627860

Table of Contents

The Jungle Book
by Rudyard Kipling

Now this is the law of the jungle,
as old and as true as the sky;
And the wolf that shall keep it may prosper,
but the wolf that shall break it must die.
As the creeper that girdles the tree trunk,
The law runneth forward and back.
For the strength of the pack is the wolf,
And the strength of the wolf is the pack.

Now this is the law of the

jungle, as old and as true

as the sky; and the wolf

that shall keep it may

prosper, but the wolf that

shall break it must die.

As the creeper that girdles

the tree trunk, the law

runneth forward and back.

For the strength of the pack is

the wolf, and the strength of

the wolf is the pack.

The Jungle Book,

by Rudyard Kipling

Tuck Everlasting
by Natalie Babbitt

*"The way I see it," Miles went on,
"It's no good hiding yourself away,
like Pa and lots of other people.
And it's no good just thinking of your
own pleasure, either. People got to
do something useful if they're going
to take up space in the world."*

"The way I see it," Miles went

on, "It's no good hiding yourself

away, like Pa and lots of other

people. And it's no good just

thinking of your own pleasure,

either. People got to do

something useful if they're

going to take up space in the

world."

Tuck Everlasting,

by Natalie Babbitt

The Wizard of Oz
by L. Frank Baum

If I ever go looking for my heart's desire again,
I won't look any further than my own back yard.
Because if it isn't there,
I never really lost it to begin with.

If I ever go looking for

my heart's desire again,

I won't look any further

than my own back yard.

Because if it isn't there,

I never really lost it

to begin with.

The Wizard of Oz,

by L. Frank Baum

The Witch of Blackbird Pond
by Elizabeth George Speare

If you ask me, it's all that schooling.
It takes the fun out of life,
being cooped up like that day after day…
Books, now that's different.
There's nothing like a book
to keep you company on a long voyage.

If you ask me, it's all that

schooling. It takes the fun out

of life, being cooped up like

that day after day... Books, now

that's different. There's

nothing like a book to keep you

company on a long voyage.

The Witch of Blackbird Pond,

by Elizabeth George Speare

Little House in the Big Woods
by Laura Ingalls Wilder

She thought to herself, "This is now."
She was glad that the cozy house,
and Pa and Ma and the fire-light and the music,
were now. They could not be forgotten,
she thought, because now is now.
It can never be a long time ago.

She thought to herself,

"This is now." She was glad

that the cozy house,

and Pa and Ma and

the fire-light and the music,

were now. They could not be

forgotten, she thought, because

now is now. It can never be a

long time ago.

Little House in the Big Woods,

by Laura Ingalls Wilder

The Lion, the Witch and the Wardrobe
by C.S. Lewis

*Peter did not feel very brave; indeed,
he felt he was going to be sick.
But that made no difference to what he had to do.*

Peter did not feel very

brave; indeed, he felt he

was going to be sick.

But that made no

difference to what

he had to do.

The Lion, the Witch

and the Wardrobe,

by C.S. Lewis

The Book of Three
by Lloyd Alexander

"By all means," cried the bard,
his eyes lighting up. "A Fflam to the rescue!
Storm the castle! Carry it by assault!
Batter down the gates!"
"There's not much of it left to storm,"
said Eilonwy.
"Oh?" said Fflewddur,
with disappointment. "Very well,
we shall do the best we can."

"By all means," cried the bard,

his eyes lighting up. "A Fflam to

the rescue! Storm the castle!

Carry it by assault! Batter

down the gates!"

"There's not much of it

left to storm," said Eilonwy.

"Oh?" said Fflewddur,

with disappointment "Very well,

we shall do the best we can."

The Book of Three,

by Lloyd Alexander

Alice in Wonderland
by Lewis Carroll

*One day Alice came to a fork in the road
and saw a cheshire cat in a tree.
"Which road do I take?" she asked.
"Where do you want to go?" was his response.
"I don't know," Alice answered.
"Then," said the cat, "it doesn't matter."*

One day Alice came to a fork in

the road and saw a cheshire

cat in a tree. "Which road

do I take?" she asked.

"Where do you want to go?"

was his response.

"I don't know," Alice answered

"Then," said the cat,

"it doesn't matter."

Alice in Wonderland,

by Lewis Carroll

Door in the Wall
by Marguerite de Angeli

"Each of us has his place in the world,"
he said. "If we cannot serve in one way
there is always another.
If we do what we are able
a door always opens to something else."

"Each of us has his

place in the world," he

said "If we cannot serve

in one way there is

always another. If we

do what we are able

a door always opens

to something else."

Door in the Wall,

by Marguerite de Angeli

20,000 Leagues Under the Sea
by Jules Verne

*The sea is everything. It covers seven tenths
of the terrestrial globe. Its breath is pure and healthy.
It is an immense desert, where man is never lonely,
for he feels life stirring on all sides.
The sea is only the embodiment of a supernatural
and wonderful existence. It is nothing but love
and emotion; it is the Living Infinite.*

The sea is everything. It
covers seven tenths of the
terrestrial globe. Its breath is
pure and healthy. It is an
immense desert, where man is
never lonely, for he feels life
stirring on all sides. The sea is

only the embodiment of a

supernatural and wonderful

existence. It is nothing but love

and emotion; it is

the Living Infinite.

20,000 Leagues Under the Sea,

by Jules Verne

Treasure Island
by Robert Lewis Stevenson

Before I had heard a dozen words,
I would not have shown myself for all the world.
I lay there, trembling and listening,
in the extreme of fear and curiosity,
for, in those dozen words,
I understood that the lives of all the
honest men aboard depended on me alone.

Before I had heard a dozen

words, I would not have shown

myself for all the world. I lay

there, trembling and listening, in

the extreme of fear and

curiosity, for, in those dozen

words, I understood that the

lives of all the honest men

aboard depended on me alone.

Treasure Island,

by Robert Lewis Stevenson

Swiss Family Robinson
by Johann David Wyss

Before us stretched a wide and lovely bay,
fringed with yellow sands, either side extending
into the distance, and almost lost to view in two shadowy
promontories; enclosed by these two arms
lay a sheet of rippling water,
which reflected in its depths the glorious sun above.
The scene inland was no less beautiful.

Before us stretched a wide

and lovely bay, fringed with

yellow sands, either side

extending into the distance,

and almost lost to view in

two shadowy promontories,

enclosed by these two

arms lay a sheet of rippling

water, which reflected in

its depths the glorious sun

above. The scene inland was

no less beautiful.

Swiss Family Robinson,

by Johann David Wyss

The Hobbit
by J.R.R. Tolkien

*If more of us valued food and cheer
and song over hoarded gold,
it would be a merrier world.*

If more of us valued food

and cheer and song over

hoarded gold, it would

be a merrier world.

The Hobbit,

by J.R.R. Tolkien

41

Rumpelstiltskin
by Wilhelm Grimm

He took her into a room
which was quite full of straw,
gave her a spinning-wheel and a reel,
and said, "Now set to work,
and if by tomorrow morning early
you have not spun this straw into gold
during the night, you must die."

He took her into a room which

was quite full of straw, gave

her a spinning-wheel and a reel,

and said, "Now set to work,

and if by tomorrow morning

early you have not spun this

straw into gold during the night,

you must die."

Rumpelstiltskin,

by Wilhelm Grimm

Pippi Longstocking
by Astrid Lindgren

"Aren't you going to dry the floor?" asked Annika.
"Oh, no, it can dry in the sun," answered Pippi.
"I don't think it will catch cold so long as it keeps moving."

"Aren't you going to

dry the floor?" asked Annika.

"Oh, no, it can dry in the sun,"

answered Pippi.

"I don't think it will

catch cold so long as

it keeps moving."

Pippi Longstocking,

by Astrid Lindgren

The Little Prince
by Antione de Saint-Exupery

Here is my secret. It is very simple:
It is only with the heart that one can see rightly;
what is essential is invisible to the eye.

Here is my secret. It is very

simple: It is only with the heart

that one can see rightly; what

is essential is invisible

to the eye.

The Little Prince,

by Antione de Saint-Exupery

Bridge to Terrabithia
by Katherine Paterson

*She had tricked him. She had made him leave
his old self behind and come into her world,
and then before he was really at home in it
but too late to go back,
she had left him stranded there - like an astronaut
wandering about on the moon. Alone.*

She had tricked him. She had

made him leave his old self

behind and come into her world,

and then before he was really

at home in it but too late to go

back, she had left him stranded

there—like an astronaut

wandering about on the moon.

Alone.

Bridge to Terrabithia,

by Katherine Paterson

Charlotte's Web
by E.B. White

"Why did you do all this for me?" he asked.
"I don't deserve it. I've never done anything for you."
"You have been my friend," replied Charlotte.
"That in itself is a tremendous thing."

"Why did you do all this for

me?" he asked. "I don't

deserve it. I've never

done anything for you."

"You have been my friend,"

replied Charlotte. "That in

itself is a tremendous thing."

Charlotte's Web,

by E.B. White

The Adventures of Robin Hood
by Howard Pyle

He who jumps for the moon, and gets it not
leaps higher than he who stoops for a penny in the mud.

He who jumps for the moon, and

gets it not leaps higher than he

who stoops for a

penny in the mud.

The Adventures of Robin Hood,

by Howard Pyle

Winnie the Pooh
by A.A. Milne

You are braver than you believe,
stronger than you seem,
smarter than you think,
and loved more than you'll ever know.

You are braver than you

believe, stronger than you

seem, smarter than you think,

and loved more than you'll

ever know.

Winnie the Pooh,

by A.A. Milne

Robinson Crusoe
by Daniel Defoe

*Thus, fear of danger is ten thousand times more terrifying
than danger itself, when apparent to the eyes;
and we find the burden of anxiety greater, by much,
than the evil which we are anxious about.*

Thus, fear of danger is

ten thousand times

more terrifying than

danger itself, when apparent to

the eyes; and we

find the burden of anxiety

greater, by much,

61

than the evil which we are

anxious about.

Robinson Crusoe,

by Daniel Defoe

The Tale of Peter Rabbit
by Beatrix Potter

Peter sat down to rest;
he was out of breath and trembling with fright,
and he had not the least idea which way to go.
Also he was very damp with sitting in that can.

Peter sat down to rest;

he was out of breath

and trembling with fright,

and he had not the least idea

which way to go.

Also he was very damp with

sitting in that can.

The Tale of Peter Rabbit,

by Beatrix Potter

The Borrowers
by Mary Norton

Mrs. May looked back at her.
"Kate," she said after a moment,
"stories never really end.
They can go on and on and on.
It's just that sometimes,
at a certain point, one stops telling them."

Mrs. May looked back at her.

"Kate," she said after a

moment, "stories never really

end. They can go on and on and

on. It's just that sometimes,

at a certain point,

one stops telling them."

The Borrowers,

by Mary Norton

Mary Poppins
by P.L. Travers

Mary Poppins gave a superior sniff.
"Don't you know," she said pityingly,
"that everybody's got a Fairyland of their own?"

Mary Poppins gave a superior

sniff. "Don't you know," she

said pityingly, "that

everybody's got a

Fairyland of their own?"

Mary Poppins,

by P.L. Travers

The Twits
by Roald Dahl

If you have good thoughts,
they will shine out of your face like sunbeams,
and you will always look lovely.

If you have good thoughts,

they will shine out of your face

like sunbeams, and you

will always look lovely.

The Twits,

by Roald Dahl

Peter Pan
by J.M. Barrie

*The moment you doubt whether you can fly,
you cease forever to be able to do it.*

The moment you doubt whether

you can fly, you cease forever

to be able to do it.

Peter Pan,

by J.M. Barrie

A Light in the Attic
by Shel Silverstein

How much good inside a day?
Depends how good you live 'em.
How much love inside a friend?
Depends how much you give 'em.

How much good inside a day?

Depends how good you live 'em.

How much love inside a friend?

Depends how much you give 'em.

A Light in the Attic,

by Shel Silverstein

Oh the Places You'll Go
by Dr. Seuss

You have brains in your head.
You have feet in your shoes.
You can steer yourself in any direction you choose.
You're on your own.
And you know what you know.
And you are the one who'll decide where to go.

You have brains in your head.

You have feet in your shoes.

You can steer yourself in any

direction you choose.

You're on your own.

And you know what you know.

And you are the one who'll

decide where to go.

Oh the Places You'll Go,

by Dr. Seuss

The Lion and the Mouse
by Aesop

No act of kindness,
no matter how small,
is ever wasted.

No act of kindness,

no matter how small,

is ever wasted.

The Lion and the Mouse,

by Aesop

A Wrinkle in Time
by Madeleine L'Engle

"They are very young.
And on their earth, as they call it,
they never communicate with other planets.
They revolve about all alone in space."
"Oh," the thin beast said. "Aren't they lonely?"

"They are very young.

And on their earth,

as they call it,

they never communicate with

other planets. They revolve

about all alone in space."

"Oh," the thin beast said.

"Aren't they lonely?"

A Wrinkle in Time,

by Madeleine L'Engle

Black Beauty
by Anna Sewell

My troubles are all over, and I am at home;
and often before I am quite awake,
I fancy I am still in the orchard at Birtwick,
standing with my friends under the apple trees.

My troubles are all over,

and I am at home;

and often before I am quite

awake, I fancy I am still in the

orchard at Birtwick, standing

with my friends under

the apple trees.

Black Beauty,

by Anna Sewell

Ready for Cursive?

Great Literature Cursive Copywork

Practice Handwriting with Excerpts from the Great Books

Experience some of the great moments in classic literature and history while improving your cursive handwriting. Copywork is the best way to learn basic grammar, spelling, and composition skills, so why practice penmanship with random words and sentences when you could be exploring amazing stories and poems by authors including:

Shakespeare	*Abraham Lincoln*
Homer	*Jane Austen*
Aristotle	*James Joyce*
Robert Frost	*Robert Louis Stevenson*
Mark Twain	*Rudyard Kipling*
Edgar Allen Poe	*…and many more*

This book includes over 40 passages. Buy online at www.speset.com.

Ready for Cursive?

Inspirational Quotes Copywork

Practice Handwriting with Inspirational Quotes from Great Leaders

Learn from the wit and wisdom of some of the greatest leaders, inventors, writers, and thinkers throughout history while improving your cursive handwriting. Copywork is the best way to learn basic grammar, spelling, and composition skills, so why practice penmanship with random words and sentences when you could be inspired by quotes about the value of hard work, education, persistence, optimism, courage, kindness, and many other virtues, in the actual words of great men and women, including:

Plato	*Winston Churchill*
Confucius	*Indira Ghandi*
Mother Teresa	*Abraham Lincoln*
Nelson Mandela	*the Dalai Lama*
Sun Tzu	*Albert Einstein*
Thomas Jefferson	*…and many more*

This book includes over 30 passages. Buy online at www.speset.com.

52940765R00052

Made in the USA
San Bernardino, CA
01 September 2017